My Favorite Houseguest

• • • • •

Mike James

FUTURECYCLE PRESS
www.futurecycle.org

Library of Congress Control Number: 2017943869

Published by FutureCycle Press
Athens, Georgia, USA

ISBN 978-1-942371-33-5

"Someone else had a bad feeling.
They will not understand the beauty of names."

Jim Brodey

• • •

"Any occasion shows the best way."

Gertrude Stein

• • • • •

"Trust me."

Paul Lynde

• • •

Contents

Gertrude Stein

Picasso said she would grow into the portrait he painted.
And she did. All the rounded spaces she filled in. Her eyes held a place in the distance, and after a while she was at that place. It did not happen quickly. It took many years. The earth turned round and round and the place came to her at last. It happened while she sat steady in her chair and sure of herself. The place was filled with flowers.

Tallulah Bankhead

If you douche with a garden hose on a neighbor's front lawn, traffic might stop. People will definitely talk. Oh, yes they will. If you call someone "Daahhling" as if it's a proper name, people will love you or hate you or call you affected or all of the above, in various stages, at once. That's probably true. Though facts shouldn't be underlined with lipstick or cocaine. They should be side by side on a table so everyone can choose.

Peter Lorre

He learned English "phonetically" to play the same character movie by movie, line by line. The wheezing accent never mattered. It was the eyes everyone noticed. They were what the cartoonists loved to draw and emphasize. The eyes said everything. Even if the whole movie was in black and white, what the eyes showed wasn't.

Bette Davis

Jimmy Baldwin loved her, said she could have been his white sister. Those song title eyes. (Hum it once, it's in your ear until bedtime.) Forget about the eyes though. Even if they seem to see you after the screen fades. Think about her voice, angry or edgy, never more pure than New York snow. It sounds like coins dropping in a slot machine, ready to play or bust.

Lewis Grizzard

There's a kosher deli in Newnan, Georgia, decorated with pictures of Lewis Grizzard and quotes of his wisdom. If you ever go to Newnan, you should look it up. It's the only kosher deli there. The potato salad is amazing. Show them this poem and see if they will give you a dollar off the lunch menu. Tell them a discount for poets and poetry lovers would make Lewis proud. Be sure to smile when you say that.

Self-Portrait, In Music

It's all cover tunes.

Dream with Sinclair Lewis

for Karen Paul Holmes

He drinks straight gin and runs his left hand through his hair.
And he sweats and sweats as if that's his only job.

The notebook he carried across two continents and at least
one state is gone. Now he is out of ideas. He's sure there were
still good ideas in his notebook, but he can't remember where
he left it.

"This is awful," he says. "Awful, awful, awful, awful." Then he looks
at me and cocks his head and takes that left hand down from
his hair.

"And why couldn't you at least be a pretty blonde," he asks.

"I know," I say. "I've asked my father the same thing."

Candy Darling

Sometimes the best-looking women are men. Because anyone can be beautiful–or at least have beautiful hair. If your name is James, it doesn't have to be. If your hair is brown, it doesn't have to stay that way. There are a thousand different people within each person. And that's just in one week.

My Closet

Thankfully, there's my closet to disappear in. I love to slide aside the hangers of flannel shirts and corduroy jackets and step in among them. Then I always shut the door to tingle in the darkness. I knot my hands together so they don't lose the absence they carry, then close my eyes and hum softly and let that sound be the only source of light in the room.

Charles Nelson Reilly

It is easy to be a character actor if you are a character. If you are not a character, but don't care to act, you can make yourself into one. If you are a character who loves to act, who harbors great ambitions, then you can make $30,000 in a month and spend $29,999. You can wear ascots and oversized glasses and speak only in double entendres. Old ladies can laugh in their daytime living rooms when you appear. They can wonder what "bad things" you do when the cameras are off. And the old ladies can wonder and wonder so much, it's a hobby for them. Even when the TV is off, they can stare at the wall so the show continues.

Character Actors from the 1950s

Kevin McCarthy was my favorite. He always looked worried
that he would say the wrong thing or maybe sweat too much.
It wasn't his eyes (too small) or his nose or lips. It was that jaw
that drew attention. Solid, like a boxer's, it punctuated his speech.
Led him from person to person, room to room, or quickly down
some small-town street. Normally, he was the fellow in the
background or a friend left loveless at a party. He was the man
who gave directions at the gas station. The banker who said "no"
to a loan. The second son his father forgot about until someone
reminded him.

Photograph of Delmore Schwartz in Central Park

The eyes are tired from looking inward. (He hasn't slept since
he was a small boy playing baseball in a vacant lot. Back then,
the dreams were not of Marx, Mann or Joyce, but of his laughing
father.) In conversation, he leans on cigarettes as though each
is a cane. So there are three mountains he climbs: boredom,
alienation, and illness. Each gets steeper with every ascent.
His steps add to his weight. He is always cold. Even in a New
York August, he wears scarf and coat. He looks as though he is
thinking, as he always is. Beside him on the bench, his pretzel
lunch sits and sits.

Andy Kaufman

It's just me. I like to have people look at me while I don't tell jokes. I've never told a joke in my life. I wouldn't know how. I can sing, just a little. I can juggle, but only with one ball at a time. And I don't throw the ball up. I throw it against a wall and see if it comes back. That's how I juggle. You can say that's not juggling, that I'm using the wrong word to describe what I do. Yeah, yeah, yeah, yeah. Now, if you'll excuse me, I'm going to make like Mighty Mouse and fly away.

Keith Haring

Everybody draws when they are little. We fall into art, get swallowed up then spit out on a sidewalk or a cornfield where some grown-up tells us to get to work and put our crayons away. There are more than 64 colors in the universe. There may be more than 640. That's something you can read on a T-shirt, which is awesome. T-shirt wisdom gets to the point. It's either profound or sentimental or it makes you laugh as you read and walk away from the person who wears it towards your destination, which might just be a Pepsi or a taco. (Love's not always around every corner.) Art should be on T-shirts as much as on museum walls. There are a lot more T-shirts than museums. That's enlightenment. Nothing is important, so everything is.

Chet Baker Blues

Say, it's just you and the night and the music and you are deep in a dream where waves invade the shore and your "old flame" looks tenderly at the almost blue of your angel eyes and says it's too late to be anyone's valentine, no matter how funny you are.

Marilyn Monroe, Dream Version

We are in the southwest desert. She looks different than in the one movie of hers I've seen (*Let's Make Love*). She's also much taller than I expected. She's very tall, and her arms are longer than they should be. Of course, since this may be my only chance, I make a move on her and let her know how attractive she is. I tell her I am a big fan. I tell her, for years, my body has ached with lust whenever I've seen a photo of her. She ignores my advances. We play ping-pong on a table beside a large cactus. Because of her height, long arms, and surprising ping-pong skills, I never score a point.

Elvis

Say the name. There's the '68 black suit. Body gorgeous, sweaty with remembered perfection. Maybe that's the best light.

Now think of the white suit and all the jokes to come. Most times, the suit is full but not bursting. It doesn't cover a man overripe with age. His stage moves don't change. The karate kick remains. The hips still pivot like a top or like a wish. The voice richer, sadder. Every third note seems held too long.

Jerry Reed

If you can sing, you are a singer. If you can dance, you are a dancer. If you can act, you are an actor. If you can do any two together, you are an entertainer. You can turn the corner in a fast car and end up in movie. The movie might be a lark, but pet rocks were larks and people still talk about them. It's a lot easier to smile at a camera than to bend all day over a guitar. Though it's hard not to smile if you hold a guitar the right way. You can shut your eyes, imagine you are strumming some woman's dark beautiful hair. Her hair warm as the sun that burns your fingers. You hold it right and don't care.

Self-Portrait with Wind and Sky

Give me a field of pristine grass untouched by man, and I'll lose interest before the next sentence. Put in a few boot tracks, tire marks, even an old beer can, and I'll perk up, start looking for people I know. Friends. Relatives. Friends of relatives. Friends of friends. Maybe that old girlfriend who always wanted sex when there were no buildings around. Let me walk in the grass. I might identify the three birds and four insects I learned, on a field trip, in fifth grade. I might start to misspeak. Call the open sky my cathedral. Find a mossy ditch to crawl in and pray.

Karl Marx

Beards are the fashion or they are not. A long beard equals commitment. It is like lifelong smoking without the cough. Beards grow and grow and mostly turn grey if they last long enough. There are theories about where the best whiskers are made. If the air is better for them in England, Paris, Belgium or Germany. To go through all the theories would take commitment and many years.

Orson Welles

At the end he is still a boy on a sled circling through snowfall. The boy has a beard and a belly and a wine jug, but he laughs like hell. No one chases him on his sled. He's fine with that. Like any good magician, his best tricks are the ones he does alone.

Letter to Jerry Falwell

Once, walking the streets of Lynchburg, VA, almost close enough to the university to hear students praying to sky, I saw a man playing a toy piano on the sidewalk. He sat on a tiny stool in front of it, not smiling at all, dressed in a three-piece suit of a style and birthmark thirty years older.

I went to a diner, there on Main Street. Had my burger and beer lunch.

The diner served home-cut fries and advice. The fries were large, finger width.

The advice was in whispers.

No one mentioned the man out front on the toy piano.
Maybe that's a common occurrence in Lynchburg where miracles are an expectation.

Bad Presidents

Are not as interesting as bad popes. People died without good reason under both, but there's less you can do in four years or eight than in twenty or thirty-five. It's like counting change to pay for lunch; that is, it's just math.

Some were not mean, but sad and small and drank too much. (Here's to you, Franklin Pierce, the Pride of New Hampshire.) Some were large-hearted and loved and trusted every man and woman in their path but, aside from card smarts, couldn't figure the job. (Warren G. Harding, anyone?)

One or two might have been great. Instead they were overcome by conspiracies seen in every cupboard, by a lack of love they could never replace. So they slumped from room to room and peeked through curtains and spoke in whispers and saw stars only through windows.

Paul Goodman

His teeth bad from ignoring them for books, boys, coffee, and thoughts. No matter. He always smiled when he gave a riposte. The listener, distracted by the bombed-out cathedral of his smile.

Footnote on Larry Eigner

"It will work as it happens," said Larry Eigner. So it will and does and happens and happens. Even if too much of a good thing is either a wonderful thing or (like too much chocolate) enough to give migraine nausea, things keep happening. Thanks be to someone high or low or nowhere in between for what Eigner, Larry Eigner, called, "the figment of man's hope."

J. R. Ewing

Some characters we only think are fiction. Then they start to walk around with us. They move into our one-bedroom apartment when we aren't looking, sleep in our beds while we are at work, and pick through the best leftovers in the fridge.

The worst don't pick up after themselves. The trashcan's mouth gapes, unable to swallow anymore. Used towels stay on the bathroom floor like commitments.

Then there is the day when a long-held lover leaves for one of them. There are those parting words, "He always knows what he wants. He never even bothers to ask."

Jack Smith Starter Kit

Be brilliant even in your dreams. Dress like a hustler or a beauty pageant winner or a fry cook, dependent on your mood. Your mood will guide you as much as your brilliance. Use great titles as bookmarks for projects left unfinished in the air or on the floor. Give up all thoughts of money or nice teeth. Perfect smiles are overrated and a twentieth century invention. Stud your vocabulary with words from trailer parks, gangster films, and symbolist poets. Build a shrine to personal masterpieces. Never leave your gas can and matches at home.

Richard Pryor

Was a muthafucka. Lived like a muthafucker. Cussed like a muthafucka. Picked stars out of the dark night like a muthafucka. Drank his blackness from a bottle like a muthafucka. Lit his ass on fire while chewing on a lion's tale and snorting up the white dust of surrender like a muthafucka. Made a joke about aforementioned fire that resulted in numerous laughter-induced pee stains for audience members around the globe. That muthafucka knew darkness so well he didn't need a flashlight. His scars gave him a map to follow. There were holes in that muthafuckin map too. Some shit he had to make up like it was real and then it was.

Ed Wood

Johnny Depp was better looking by much. There's no bias in the opinion of experts. Still, here's the thing: really bad can be extra special. If tackiness creates an aesthetic (see Miami in spring or any season), so does pure awfulness.

An interstate billboard off Highway 70 advertises, *The World's Worst Fried Chicken.* And it might be. All grease and gristle.

Some movies are only as good as that chicken. Those taped-together paper plates that fly across the screen, kite string visibly attached, are called spaceships. They don't fly as high as a billboard. They barely go higher than a rooster in full flutter.

Everyday American Magus

for Christopher Harter

Harry Smith claimed he once held the philosopher's stone but
lost it in the boroughs of New York. He described his adventures
in self-drawn comics, also currently lost. Along the way, he
collected paper airplanes. Collected them from street corners,
school yards and trash cans. Collected lots of them. His collection
is now at the Smithsonian Institution, 600 Maryland Avenue SW,
Washington, DC 20002. He loved music, especially the found
kind. His *Anthology of American Folk Music* made him famous
but not rich. He recorded birds in Central Park, the oral histories
of jump rope rappers, and the favorite jokes of six-year-olds.
All with handheld recorders. Of course, he liked to paint.
He painted urine-stained oil portraits and destroyed them.
He made magic silent films and threw them away. He wrote
masterful, surreal formalist verse on unsent postcards, bedsheets,
collection notices, hotel room walls and Chinese takeout menus.
No one ever published a collection of his poems. He liked to drink
and take drugs and did both and well. He never had sex with
either a man or a woman. He often scratched his old records while
playing them. He gave most of his records away. Allen Ginsberg
once took a photo of Harry Smith transforming milk into milk.
Such are the gifts of alchemy.

Stan Brakhage

What's out of focus stays that way. Call it abstraction. Though it's really movement. The blur is something happening. It's life without clean lines.

Show a hand shuffling a deck of cards. Not two hands. One. Show another hand with a cheap engagement ring and green painted nails. Let that hand draw a card. Someone can say a few words or not.

Billy Strayhorn

Romance is mush, especially on the road. There are needs, though. Go right down beneath the bone. Some things are more sociable than hellos. Certainly more appreciated. The last song ends and where do you go? Back to the hotel for a drink or a smoke. Walk the late night to see what a park bench brings. Sit with a blanket of stars amid joy and release.

Steve McQueen

Shaggy eyes make people think you are better than you are. Smarter. More soulful. Sometimes that's enough. If you look tough, then people think you are tough. It's easier to be dumb if you have an English accent. Who doesn't know that? But that's about sound. I'm talking about just looking and standing in place, trying to let the world know what you are thinking even if you aren't thinking too much. Isn't that funny? You can prepare for a scene by finding one good thought to hold onto.

Sal Mineo

Yes, that Sal Mineo, was never mistaken for Pat Boone. His fleshly fingers seldom carried a Bible, even as a prop. His face all lips and eyes. He started out doing what he was told, then gave that up. Said enough and did what he wanted as much as he could from there until the end. He loved who he loved and said so before others did or said. He did what he wanted as much as he could.

David Carradine

Death is a rumor that keeps getting verified. There's nothing profound about saying the truth. If I walk backwards and say my lines, I probably won't say them as well as if I walk forward. It's less natural to go in reverse. That's ok. Death's out in front of us. It's that roadblock we can't walk around.

John Wayne

Loved Tolkien and hated horses. How many would bet the reverse? As much an invention as any cowboy or soldier he played. He believed in midnight, bourbon, and tomorrow. Walked slow and talked slow across plains and desert. He gave up being Marion to become John Wayne. His second name, two single syllables, said quickly, like a bullet, or stretched out like a yell in a valley.

Nixon

Some fathers are just bad. Drink too much. Gamble with money set aside for school shoes. Wear a five-o'clock shadow all day over pale sweat. Make bad jokes to their daughter's teenage friends. And lie. Lie out of habit and grief. Because their lips are moving. Because truly, truly they can think of nothing else to say.

Self Portrait, In a Dream

I am in my house with a bb gun. The North Koreans have attacked once again. I spend all of my time looking out the back window and counting canned goods in the kitchen closet. Even though it´s daylight and power is on in the house, it is very dark. Fear keeps everything in place. None of the shadows are mobile.

Interviews with Famous Men

A man at the next table is holding a banana and talking to himself. He's not holding the banana like a phone. He is holding it in place at his table, with both hands, like he is afraid the banana will forget gravity, just float away.

The man is also staring at a reproduction of Custer's Last Stand. The picture's been on the coffee shop wall for years. Not as faded as it could be. No random graffiti artist has doodled horns on top of Custer's golden locks or added historical commentary. Maybe the man is thinking of such random graffiti. Maybe he is not talking to himself, but talking to the picture. If he is, I hope the picture talks back. I hope, in his afterlife, Custer opened a salon.

This Fellow, Jack, Not Famous, But a Friend

Large in every way. Large hands, large head, large beard, large belly. Worked, now and then, as taxi driver, teacher, toll collector, archaeologist and, oh yes, postal worker. Owned exactly six Hawaiian shirts. No matter the weather, was never cold. Liked Spanish and Shakespeare, jazz and dirty jokes. Liked obscurity in everything, but language. Liked children, noisy ones most of all. Liked women. Liked women a lot. Never had money, nope, not ever. Lived in a rented house with few windows, three lawn chairs and a wealth of books. Favorite books included: *Under the Sign of Saturn, The Empire City* and *Kingsblood Royal.* Collected postcards from nearly everywhere. Hand-rolled all his many, many cigarettes. Lived on coffee, fish sandwiches, friends and poetry.

Willard Maas

If your wife is a genius and your best friend is a genius, what does that make ambitious you? Lonely. We tell bad jokes to get to good ones. Go through a role of film for one nice shot. Write a thousand bad lines for half-a-dozen that work together.

Those who can't write as well as others can sometimes drink all the better. Arthur said some people drink because they aren't poets. What about those who drink because they almost are?

David Wojnarowicz

Even with practice, some names are hard. Let your tongue
roll around like it's on a sidewalk or a brick wall, like it's finding
your way down an alley or up some half-painted back stairs.
At best your pronunciation will be close, your accent off.
Even if you say the name backwards and your mouth exhales
into the kiss of an o.

Marie Menken

Worked as a secretary. Was the only genius in her marriage.

Basquiat

I start a picture and finish it. I hide my name in there or else the name I feel like for that day. The more I paint the more I like everything. As a kid my drawings were abstract and awful. I can actually draw. I know that now. I've known it for a long time. Just because you are a painter doesn't mean everyone thinks you can draw. I have Coltrane or Hendrix in my head when I am moving the brush. That sounds fake because it is. A lot of times I'm like a pilot on the runway, all clear. That's why kids make the best artists. They start from nowhere. We are all trying to get back there.

Nude Descending a Staircase, No. 2

She thinks no one is watching, but she doesn't take her time.
She's all movement. Where she was is already gone. Her last step
not quite as far away as yesterday, but already in the large house
of the past. Her descent is not a performance. She thinks no one
is watching. Her descent is an act of becoming. Somewhere
a mathematician dreams her. In the dream she is motionless,
a constant of angles and curves.

Unembellished Facts

Wayne only painted on white umbrellas. Not stretched canvas. Not framed cardboard. Not cut wood. Not sliced metal. Not on any walls where Kilroy lived. Not even beneath bridges, for every tourist and commuter to see.

Wayne was steadfast, refused to use anything other than washable paint. Said, only it holds the light.

Wayne had one wealthy patron who loved umbrella art and penny fountains and a few other things he never thought to mention. This patron always visited and bought in the rainy season.

At night, Wayne dreamed of beaches with tall sand castles and taller waves. He dreamed of crossing the ocean in an upturned umbrella, the water a blue reflection of sky.

Every morning, Wayne drank coffee out of a saucer. Said saucers look like open umbrellas. Yes, he did.

Warren Zevon

Had a city for a soul and a big one. There were slums and business districts and places set aside for gentrification. There was more than one farmer's market where all the sellers "grew their own." There was a red light district, exotic and friendly. It was not as large as most of the other districts and, certainly, not as large as many would have thought. The Jewish district covered two blocks, Chinatown sixteen. A walker could go from one city end to the other if he left at first light with strong legs and didn't use too much breath saying hello to every passing stranger.

In Bob Dylan's Neighborhood

It's hard to get Johnny out of the basement. He likes it there with his books and chemistry. If he were a pharmacist, he'd mix up medicine. If he were an alchemist, he'd try to make gold. Johnny's just a big kid with a chemistry set. He used to work at the factory. Now he's a laid-off genius, smart as Aquinas. He stays in his basement with his potions and books. Johnny won't walk the pavement and the alleyways. He won't talk about the government. Says it just is. It's hard to get Johnny out of the basement, even to go see Maggie (his once and only love) who is always soot-faced from her job and always talking and talking about leaving town for good. She says Brownville is not for her or for anyone with anything close to a soul. Maggie wants a place in the country, too small to even be called a farm, where she can wear sandals all day and use candles as the evening's only light. She says it's evening year-round in some places where the sky is always dark or getting there.

John Ritter

Tex Ritter, star of country music and cowboy movies, knew how to yodel and yodel and lasso with the best of them. But who cares about him? His lasso wasn't magic like Wonder Woman's.
Tex Ritter never flew an invisible plane.

Let's introduce Tex's son, John.

To play gay in 1970s sitcom America was to flip a wrist and sway. Perhaps arch an eyebrow. Roll the eyes. Hint at knowledge an audience might giggle over. Then let them giggle and snort.

In *Sling Blade,* which premiered almost 20 years after *Three's Company* first aired, John Ritter played a character who was gay, not pretending. The character was never flamboyant, just hesitant. His smile was broken. There were shadows, that weren't mascara, around his eyes.

Lou Reed

When his parents sent him for electroshock, he probably wished they loved him a little more or a little less. He said it was for urges he took care of later at Warhol's Factory. No one was shocked by anything there. Andy might say, "Oh, gee." In no world is that phrase a condemnation. It's hard to even say it with an exclamation, especially if you are thinking about Andy and about how he talked, which was so different from how Lou talked. Lou was deadpan, but emphatic. Didn't matter if was quoting Baudelaire or saying late Elvis (not early Elvis) was barely better than static.

Alfred Starr Hamilton

No room in a rooming house is ever palace-like, even in Montclair, New Jersey. Paint the walls lavender or leave them winter bare, they are still no more than two arm's length and three butterfly wings from one to another.

Take a thermos of tea on your early evening walk. So what if kids across the street make fun of a weather bit coat and a bread crumb trail of pigeons. You don't have to close your eyes or leave the sidewalk to dance on the moon as a stranger.

Self-Portrait

I am alone, face up, in a canoe. As I go steadily down the river,
I can see nothing but sky and clouds and an occasional spray
of water and foam. I listen for voices or drums or birds. All I can
hear is the water. I'm wearing only white socks and a *Yankees* hat.
If I could just move my arms, I know I could fly.

How Poets Die

Fall off a barstool, jump from a bridge, fail to dodge beach-
roving dune buggy in the dark, walk headfirst into speeding Buick,
contract syphilis and lose marbles first, contract AIDS from holding
love hard and in secret, drink and drink, snort something or shoot
it up, old-age-happy in bed (that's the best, of course), pine
away for what's not there, grow thin from hunger, find words
not enough.

Andy Warhol

The wig got itchy under runway lights. The great thing about a runway is everyone can feel deeply superficial or sexy or feel like a machine, which is almost like bliss since a machine feels nothing at all. Some people forget emotions and never remember them again. They think that's ordinary, and maybe it is because so many people do that. Maybe that's the most ordinary thing. A plastic cup is ordinary and almost no one notices it. Look at anything long enough and all the meaning falls away.

• • •

• • • • •

• • •

Acknowledgments

Some of the poems in this collection have appeared, sometimes in different versions, in the following magazines:

Abbey: "Basquiat"
Asheville Poetry Review: "Warren Zevon," "Photograph of Delmore Schwartz In Central Park"
Dead Snakes: "Andy Warhol," "Dream with Sinclair Lewis," "Karl Marx"
First Literary Review-East: "Keith Haring," "Paul Goodman"
Green Panda: "This Fellow, Jack"
Kentucky Review: "John Wayne," "David Carradine"
Laurel Review: "In Bob Dylan's Neighborhood"
Main Street Rag: "Letter to Jerry Falwell"
Misfit: "Jerry Reed," "How Poets Die"
Philadelphia Poets: "Character Actors from the 1950s"
Skidrow Penthouse: "Gertrude Stein," "Peter Lorre," "Tallulah Bankhead"
Third Wednesday: "Jack Smith," "David Wojnarowicz," "Elvis"
Uppagus: "Candy Darling," "My Closet"
Verse Wisconsin: "Everyday American Magus"
Your One Phone Call: "Nixon"

Cover artwork by Heather Symmes; cover and interior book design by Diane Kistner; Avenir text and Bodega Sans Black titling

About FutureCycle Press

FutureCycle Press is dedicated to publishing lasting English-language poetry books, chapbooks, and anthologies in both print-on-demand and Kindle ebook formats. Founded in 2007 by long-time independent editor/publishers and partners Diane Kistner and Robert S. King, the press incorporated as a nonprofit in 2012. A number of our editors are distinguished poets and writers in their own right, and we have been actively involved in the small press movement going back to the early seventies.

The FutureCycle Poetry Book Prize and honorarium is awarded annually for the best full-length volume of poetry we publish in a calendar year. Introduced in 2013, our Good Works projects are anthologies devoted to issues of universal significance, with all proceeds donated to a related worthy cause. Our Selected Poems series highlights contemporary poets with a substantial body of work to their credit; with this series we strive to resurrect work that has had limited distribution and is now out of print.

We are dedicated to giving all of the authors we publish the care their work deserves, making our catalog of titles the most diverse and distinguished it can be, and paying forward any earnings to fund more great books.

We've learned a few things about independent publishing over the years. We've also evolved a unique, resilient publishing model that allows us to focus mainly on vetting and preserving for posterity poetry collections of exceptional quality without becoming overwhelmed with bookkeeping and mailing, fundraising activities, or taxing editorial and production "bubbles." To find out more about what we do, come see us at www.futurecycle.org.

The FutureCycle Poetry Book Prize

All full-length volumes of poetry published by FutureCycle Press in a given calendar year are considered for the annual FutureCycle Poetry Book Prize. This allows us to consider each submission on its own merits, outside of the context of a contest. Too, the judges see the finished book, which will have benefitted from the beautiful book design and strong editorial gloss we are famous for.

The book ranked the best in judging is announced as the prize-winner in the subsequent year. There is no fixed monetary award; instead, the winning poet receives an honorarium of 20% of the total net royalties from all poetry books and chapbooks the press sold online in the year the winning book was published. The winner is also accorded the honor of being on the panel of judges for the next year's competition; all judges receive copies of all contending books to keep for their personal library.

Made in the USA
Middletown, DE
03 July 2017